I found it to be an excellent tool that can be used in understanding what Scripture has to say about God and the family. It was nice to be able to have it pulled together in one resource.

Jeff Cochran
President and CEO of In Christ Athletics

1. This is a very profound book that goes in depth on each subject; even a young child can comprehend what's being said.

2. The word of GOD is spoken and written in a way that doesn't offend you, brings condemnation nor causes you to fall into disbelief, but it causes you to think about things in a way that you NEVER had before

3. When I first read the words, the introduction of the book caught my attention. And, if the intro doesn't get me, then I may not even finish reading the book

4. Knitting the family closer together today is such a task. Many of us are such workaholics that we miss out on our children and that is not what GOD intended. Being a single mother with multiple children caused me to have to work, School and even get a second job if needed.

-Tawania Dodd

THE FAMILY BIBLE STUDY SERIES

Family Bible Studies

Part One: The Family of God—Foundation

Guidelines in the Scriptures for discovering the foundation
for the family, character development and family stability.

Eric C. Dohrmann

WESTBOW
PRESS®
A DIVISION OF THOMAS NELSON
& ZONDERVAN

Guidelines in the Scriptures for discovering the foundation for the family, character development and family stability.

WestBow Press books may be ordered through booksellers or by contacting:

WestBow Press
A Division of Thomas Nelson & Zondervan
1663 Liberty Drive
Bloomington, IN 47403
www.westbowpress.com
1 (866) 928-1240

ISBN: 978-1-4908-6240-8 (sc)
ISBN: 978-1-4908-6241-5 (e)

Library of Congress Control Number: 2014921798

Printed in the United States of America.

WestBow Press rev. date: 11/20/2015

Contents

To the Trinity...Who helps bring us harmony in all we do

Preface

The demand on our time and schedules in today's day and age is very great. The pace of life seems to have picked up since previous generations. Some days on the job can be overwhelming with continual pressures to get things done. Then some days at home you can have so much to deal with that it becomes hard to even get the daily priorities accomplished. I would say that these pressures are especially true and felt by parents of today. With most children attending school outside the home for their education and most often with both parents working these days, seeing the children during the daytime is rare. When everyone finally arrives back home, night activities can fill up fast for the remaining hours. Meals to cook, housecleaning to maintain, various outside events, some playtime and homework for the children, plus a variety of entertainment and relaxing interests for family members can make it nearly impossible for the family to spend any time together. Weekends can be much the same way unless family time together is planned out otherwise. The choice for children to take time to be with the family instead of their desire to be with personal friends can be quite a tough decision of values for them to make, also. Parents must set up the most important priorities for the family to live by as well as the plan for how to carry them out.

Without the instruction, training, and discipline of the Lord passed down from parents, children can go astray. (In Proverbs 29:18, the word *vision* is the word for prophecy, and it references the revelation of the Lord and the Bible.) Yet with the foundation of God's guidelines in His Word and the training and discipline given to them, hope and promise from the Lord is given to them and their futures (Prov. 22:6; Isa. 55:6–11; Matt. 24:35).

This book is the first of a three-part series of books intended to help individuals and parents accomplish this goal. The series theme is "growing in the family of God" and centers on personal and collective development for the whole family. It uses God's guidelines taken right from the Bible with a focus on the book of Proverbs and other related Bible passages. This first book of the Family Bible Study series, *The Foundation of the Family of God*, presents the biblical foundation for the family past, present, and future. The second book will focus on relationships, discovering the different levels that exist. The third book will center on growing in God's wisdom, building on the first two books and pressing on to maturing in our daily walk with the Lord.

Parents have the sole responsibility to bring up their children in the instruction, training, and discipline of the Lord (Eph. 6:4; Prov. 22:6). This book series has been designed to help individuals, parents, and expecting parents to become efficient in spending and utilizing their time together with their family or group in family Bible study. The format is simple and direct. Read and share the Scriptures with the children or group and discuss with them ways to apply them in their lives.

Hearing God's Word being read and discussing it with their children is the basic beginning and foundation for parents to help their children make the Holy Scriptures the standard for their lives. This is what children especially need to see and hear, and most importantly, this needs to be modeled for them by their parents. The most important priority for parents is simple (carried out in these three books)-- to read relevant Scripture passages with the family and help them discuss, choose, and apply those Scriptures as the standard for their lives (Prov. 22:6; Isa. 55:6–11; Matt. 24:35).

The Preface all the way to the section titled Parental Instructors detail the foundational elements of the family for parents. These include the definitions of family, the character and functions of the Trinity, commentary on creation and the first family in the Garden of Eden (Gen. 1–4), and God's design and the role for parents. The section titled Other Models of God for His Children begins the Bible study with the family.

For each of these selected topics, read over all the Scripture passages for your own personal study first. In doing so, ask yourself these two basic questions: "What is God wanting us to learn in this passage of the Bible?" Always consider the context in your reading, namely the verses before and after what you are reading. Then ask, "How does this apply to my own life?" Ask God before you begin your study to direct you in your answers (and the answers to other questions you may have). The context within the passage will reveal what God is saying and what He wants us to know about that Scripture. Then pray about what He wants us to apply in our lives.

Take the same approach with your family. Where there are a number of Scripture passages listed to read within a topic, pick out (circle or note) the passages most relevant to your family's concerns and needs. Most of the passages are short (except some of the narratives) and do not take long to read. Read the passages and discuss together the same two questions that you applied to yourself. Let others ponder their answers as they think out and share their thoughts. When finished, ask God to guide and help you work out applying these in your lives. Once you start the studies, have the children or group members share how any previous studies have become relevant and helped them in their personal lives. New insights may come out in sharing these with one another.

As we can now see, time can be spent with the family or group members, reading, discussing, and sharing how to apply God's Word in our lives together. Indeed, it will be time well spent with one another, keeping in mind both God's past, present and future promises, reading and sharing together His eternal word (Matt. 24:35). Spending time to apply (live out) these discoveries together would then be the next beneficial step. Consider Jesus' discipleship process and the training that He did with the apostles. Now we can see for ourselves more of what the whole process involves—getting together to read, hear, discuss, and apply God's Word to our lives. In the process we are becoming examples and models to others as we learn to daily live out His Word in our lives.

Introduction

The eternal family of God has always existed—the Father (Gen. 21:33; Isa. 40:28; John 17:3), the Son (John 1:1; 17:3; 1 John 5:20), and the Holy Spirit (2 Cor. 3:17; Heb. 9:14), also known as the Trinity. Together they decided to expand their family by creating humankind in the image of God (Gen. 1:26). Placed in the Garden of Eden on earth with God present with them (Gen. 3:8), man and his helper (woman) broke the prohibited command that God gave them (Gen. 2:16, 17; 3:6) and were put out of the garden (Gen. 3:24). But God gave them the promise of the seed that would one day crush the head of the Serpent, Satan, and bring the hope of God's redemption to humankind (Gen. 3:15; Gal. 3:16), fulfilled in God the Son, Jesus Christ. As the promise continued to grow through Abraham and God's chosen people, Israel, until fulfilled in Jesus Christ, God gave this remarkable promise to Abraham. Through Abraham's seed all nations of the earth would be blessed (Gen. 18:18; 22:18; 28:14; Gal. 3:8, 16). In Acts 3:25 (NASB), Peter quotes this verse in his message spoken to the people of Israel, saying, "And in your seed all the families of the earth shall be blessed." Following this promise through the New Testament, this will have its ultimate fulfillment and completion in the new heaven and new earth that God makes for all eternity that His family will enjoy forever (Rev. 21–22:5).

This Bible study guide on Family of God will lay the foundation and help you enjoy discovering God's design, plan, fulfillment, and applications for God's family. We will see through the Scriptures the Godhead as our model and guide for family living on earth and forever in eternity.

As you read along, look up each Scripture verse included with each topic and write down any helpful insights you have. It is not an exhaustive study but includes some of the basic designs, guidelines, and practical applications you can draw from the Bible (Matt. 24:35; 2 Tim. 3:16, 17). The main focus is on the family as a unit and how the Trinity, the eternal family of God, sets for us and leads us as our example and model for the family, now and forever, individually and collectively as a family unit.

With the longer lists of the Scripture verses at the end of the study, room has been made to check off the passages as you follow along and write down your discoveries when you read them. Some topics have various dimensions to their understanding (concept) and even wider varieties of applications. These Scriptures can help numerous people with different experiences and circumstances they face. It will make it easy to follow where you leave off and where you pick up for your next study as you write down your own discoveries. I have used the New American Standard Bible version for the basis of my study.

Basic Definitions

Let's begin first with basic definitions.

What is a family? Family is defined as the basic unit in society, traditionally consisting of two parents rearing their children. Merriam-Webster's Collegiate Dictionary, 11th edition, 2013, also makes reference to any various social units differing from but regarded as equivalent to the traditional family, such as a single-parent family.

Family in the New Testament is categorized by two words:

1. *Oikos*—A dwelling; a house; a household; family.
2. Patria—Similar to the word *pater*, meaning father; ancestry; linage; a family or tribe; in a wider sense, nationalities and race (see Acts 3:25).

What is a father? Father is defined as a man who has begotten a child; a male parent; ancestor; the first person of the Trinity (Merriam-Webster's Collegiate Dictionary, 11th edition, 2013).

The word *father* is taken from a root word signifying a nourisher; a protector; upholder; spiritual fathers through the gospel (1 Cor. 4:15); God as Father of His children. They become imitators of their

Father (Matt. 5:44, 45, 48) and trust Him for their rewards and needs (Matt. 6).

What is a mother? Mother is defined as a female parent (as a noun); to give birth to; to care for or protect like a mother (as a verb; Merriam-Webster's Collegiate Dictionary, 11th edition, 2013; see 2 Tim. 1:5.)

Theme Verse of the Study

Ephesians 3:14–15 says, "For this reason I bow my knees before the Father, from whom every family in heaven and on earth derives its name." (NASB)

Here the passage references the family of God in heaven and on earth, those whom the Father draws (John 6:44) and brings about their birth into His family (John 1:12, 13). This is a "reference to all those who are spiritually related to God the Father. He is the author of their spiritual relationship with Him as His children, and they are united to one another in family fellowship" (Vine's Expository Dictionary, under the word family).

Let's look at the context of Ephesians relating to this verse. In chapter 1, Paul mentions our adoption as sons into God's family through Jesus (v. 5), sealed with the Holy Spirit of promise (v. 13), given as a pledge toward our redemption of God's own possession (v. 14), according to the kind intention of His will (vs.5, 9). By His great love and mercy (Eph. 2:4), He saved us from being sons of disobedience (Eph. 2:2; 5:6) to be walking with Him in good works and growing as imitators of Him as His beloved children (Eph. 2:10; 5:1, 2). He broke down the barrier between Jew and Gentile (Eph. 2:14) and now makes the two into one new man in Christ (Eph. 2:13–16). Both now have access to the Father through the Spirit (Eph. 2:18). As fellow citizens of God's household, the whole building is being built into a holy temple (Eph.

2:21) as they are being built together into a dwelling place of God in the Spirit (Eph. 2:22).

In the beginning of chapter 3, Paul reminds the Ephesians of the stewardship God gave him for them. The word stewardship here combines two words in the original language to mean 'a manager of a household'. Because people have passed on to them the gospel and God's grace extended to the Gentiles, they have now become joint heirs and members of Christ's body, by the promise in Christ through the gospel (Eph. 3:6; 1:9–14; John 10:16).

The Eternal Family of God—The Trinity

The eternal family is the Trinity, the family of the Godhead, the Father, the Son, and the Holy Spirit. They are the three persons in the one God. They have the same nature but different functions. Yet in their different functions they can and usually do assist one another in Their work, as the Bible reveals, and they always work together in complete harmony. Here are some examples: Gen. 1:26; 3:22; 11:7; Job 33:4; Col. 1:16; John 3:34; 14:15–17, 23, 25, 26; 15:26; 16:13–15; 1 Cor. 12:3–7; 2 Cor. 1:21, 22; Eph. 2:17–22; 3:14–19; 4:3–7; Heb. 9:13, 14; 1 John 3:21–24; Rev. 4 and 5.

Let's look at some of the characteristics of the Trinity.

Eternal—This means without beginning or end (Gen. 21:33; Ps. 90:1, 2; Isa. 40:28; 57:15; John 17:3; Heb. 9:14; 1 John 5:20).

Holy—Moral perfection; complete (Lev. 19:2; Deut. 32:4; Isa. 40:25, 26; Isa. 57:15; Matt. 5:48; 1 Thess. 4:8; Heb. 4:15; 7:26; Rev. 4:8).

Infinite—Unlimited existence, capacity, energy, and perfection (Ps. 90:1, 2; 147:5; Isa. 40:28; Matt. 5:48; Rom. 11:33–36; Heb. 1:3).

Love—Unconditional (for who we are, not just for what we have done) (Ex. 34:6, 7; 1 Kings 10:9; Ps. 25:6; Ps. 136; Jer. 33:11; Lam. 3:22, 23; Matt. 5:43–48; John 3:14–17; 1 John 4:8, 16).

Omnipotent—All-powerful (Gen. 17:1; Job 33:4; Isa. 51:15; Heb. 1:1–3; Rev. 1:8; 15:3).

Omnipresent—All-present (Ps. 139:7–12; Jer. 23:23, 24).

Omniscient—All-knowing (Ps. 147:5; Isa. 40:28; 1 John 3:19, 20).

Perfect—Complete (Deut. 32:4; Matt. 5:48; James 1:17).

Self-Sufficient—Self-existing within one's own eternal nature (Gen. 21:33; Isa. 40:28, 29; Mal. 3:6; Col. 1:15–17; Heb. 1:1–3).

Spirit—As opposed to material (John 4:24).

Triune—Existing as a personal nature in three persons (three persons in one God).

Truth—That which is in agreement with the facts; the characteristics of God that tell us He is real and exists (Deut. 32:4; Ps. 31:3–5; Isa. 45:19; 65:16; Jer. 10:10; John 1:14–18; 14:6, 16, 17; 15:26; 16:13; 17:3; Rom. 1:20; 1 Tim. 3:14–16; 1 John 5:20).

Creator of All Things—Creation of all things out of nothing (Gen. 1:1, 2; 1:26, 27, 31; Job 33:4; Ps. 8:3–5; 19:1–6; 24:1, 2; 90:1, 2; Ps. 104; Isa. 40:21–26; 42:5; Jer. 10:12; 32:17; John 1:1–3, 10; Col. 1:16, 17; Heb. 1:1–3; 11:1–3; Rev. 4:11).

Functions of the Triune God

God the Father—God the Father rules and reigns upon His throne in heaven over all His creation and kingdom (Ps. 11:4; 47:5–9; 103:19–22; Isa. 40:21, 22; Dan. 7:9, 10, 13, 14; Rev. 4:2, 3; 5:1, 7, 13). He is the owner, Father, and vinedresser of the church and prunes His vineyard (church) so it will produce its designed fruit (Matt. 21:33–44; John 15:1, 2; James 5:7). He gave His Son, Jesus, to be the Savior of the world from their sins (Matt. 1:18–23; Luke 2:8–14; John 3:13–17; 1 Tim. 4:10; 1 John 2:1, 2; 4:14). And to all who believe and receive Jesus, the Savior, they come to know the Trinity and receive eternal life (John 1:1, 2, 12–14, 18; 3:16; 14:16, 17, 23; 17:3; Acts 4:12; Rom. 6:23; 2 Cor. 6:16–18). He will restore heaven and earth with a new heaven and earth so that God may dwell together with His people forever (Isa. 65:17–19; 2 Peter 3:9-13; Rev. 21:1–7).

God the Son—Jesus Christ, God the Son, is God's Messiah and Savior to the world (1 Chron. 17:10–14; Ps. 2; 16:10; 40;6–8; Ps. 110; Isa. 7:14; 9:6, 7; 42:1–4; 52:13–53:12; Jer. 23;5, 6; Dan. 7:13, 14; Mic. 5:2–5; Zech. 12:10–14; Matt. 1:18–23; 16:16; John 1:1, 2, 14, 18; 4:25, 26; 10:30; Col. 2:9; Heb. 1:1–3; 1 John 5:20). He was sent to accomplish God's purposes and fulfill the Scriptures written about Him (Gen. 3:15; 22:18; Gal. 3:16; Luke 24:44–47; John 17:1–4; 19:24, 36; Acts 2:25–36; Eph. 1:9, 10; 1 Peter 1:10–12). He was with the Father before the creation of the world, and He is the Creator of all things (John1:1–3, 10; 8:58; 17:5, 24; Col. 1:15–17; Heb. 1:2; Rev. 4:11; Gen. 1:1, 2; Job 33:4).

These verses show us the harmony and compatibility of the Trinity in creation. He came to earth to reveal who God is (John 1:1, 2, 14–18; 5:18, 19; 10:30; 14:9–11; Col. 1:15, 19; Heb. 1:1–3). He came to destroy the Devil's works (John 12:31; 16:8–11; 1 Cor. 15:54–57; 1 John 3:4–9). And He will be God's judge of humankind (Matt. 28:18; John 3:16–21; 5:21–30; 17:2; 2 Tim. 4:1), and He will be the conquering King when He returns to earth to rule and reign in His kingdom, which will never end (Dan. 2:44; 7:13, 14; Matt. 25:34; Luke 1:26–33; 1 Cor. 15:23–28; Rev. 1:4–6; 5; 17:14; 19:1–21; 20:4–6; 22:5).

The Holy Spirit—God The Holy Spirit is the promised gift to those who believe in Jesus and His sacrificial death on the cross for their sins and His bodily resurrection from the dead (2 Cor. 3:17, 18; Luke 24:49; John 14:16, 17; Acts 1:4, 5; 2:22–39). He comes into the life of those who believe in Jesus and receive Him into their lives as their Savior and Lord (John 1:12, 13; 3:3–6; 14:15–17, 20; Acts 2:38, 39). God seals the believer and gives the Holy Spirit as a pledge (down payment) of our inheritance in Christ (John 6:27; 2 Cor. 1:21, 22; 5:5; Eph. 1:13, 14). He guides the believer into all truth and reveals future things to come (Luke 4:1–14; John 14:17, 26; 15:26; 16:13; Isa. 11:2; Rev. 1:10; 4:2; 17:3; 21:10). Future prophecies in the book of Revelation were given to John to complete the Scriptures, revealing the end of time. He convicts the world of sin, righteousness, and judgment (John3:16–21; 16:8–11). He develops and demonstrates the inner character of God within the believer (John 3:34; 14:16, 17, 23; 1 Cor. 13; 2 Cor. 1:3–5; Gal. 5:22–25; 2 Peter 1:2–8), and outward signs, wonders, miracles, and leadership character giftings come through the distribution of His spiritual gifts (Acts 2:22, 43; 6:3–5, 10; 14:14; 15:12; Rom. 12:3–8; 15:18, 19; 1 Cor. 12:1–11; Eph. 4:11–13; Heb. 2:2–4). He continues to exhort the world through the church to receive God's gift of salvation (John 3:16, 17; 16:7–11; Acts 1:6–8; 2:38, 39; 1 Peter 1:10–12; Rev. 21:5–7; 22:17).

The First Family on Earth

All things are centered on the family since all things have been created by the eternal family, the Trinity, the family of the Godhead. (Even solar systems, which are families of stars and planets like ours, are being discovered today through the use of modern technology.) The Trinity works in complete harmony, and Their creation of the universe, earth, and humankind—made in the image of God—are great examples. What beautiful examples they are at that! (Gen. 1, 2, 26, 31; Job 33:4; John 1:1, 2; Col. 1:15–17; Rev. 4:11; Prov. 8:22-31; Job 38–41).

In the first three days of creation God made designs for the earth. Day one brought the night and day (Gen. 1:3–5). On day two He created the expanse in the atmosphere, the sky (Gen. 1:6–8). On day three He gathered the waters (the seas) for dry ground to appear and vegetation (plants, trees, and fruit) to grow (Gen. 1:9–13). In the next three days God began to fill up what was made in the first three days (Gen. 1:14–31). This included man and woman being made in the image of God on day six (Gen. 1:26, 27). The word for *image* means resemblance, a representative figure (see also Heb. 10:5; Ps. 40:6). This leads us to the possible thought that the creation of our physical bodies were made from (or like) the physical body that Jesus would have when He would come to earth—that is, the body Jesus would have was already decide before man was created. Thus, our bodies were then actually formed to be like His (see John 1:14-18; Heb. 4:3; 10:1–10; Gen. 3:8; 18:33).

Beginning in Genesis 2:7, God expands on His creation of man and woman, whom He made in His image. In two separate creations, God first formed the man from the earth (his physical nature) and then breathed life into him (his spiritual nature). The man became a living being (Gen. 2:7). He put man in the beautiful Garden of Eden and provided food from the plants and trees for him to eat (Gen. 1:29–31; 2:8, 9). The only restriction was that he could not eat from the Tree of Knowledge of Good and Evil, lest he would die (Gen. 2:16, 17).

As in the example of the Trinity, it was not good for man to be alone with his responsibilities over God's creation (Gen. 1:26–28; 2:18–20). After He created all the animals on earth and birds in the sky and man gave names to them all, no helper for man was found for him (Gen. 2:19, 20). So, in a separate creation, God created a helper in His image for man (Gen. 1:27). Word for *helper* means aid. It comes from the Hebrew verb to surround, protect, or aid.

Taking one of man's ribs, God fashioned it into a woman (Gen. 2:21–25; 1 Peter 3:7). Now made of the same bone and flesh, they shall come together to become one. Physically they are made of the same nature (flesh). Spiritually God gives them the breath of life since He is a spirit (John 4:24). Their purpose was to rule over—that is, bring under control—all the animals, creatures, and plants on earth and to multiply on the earth (Gen. 1:28; 9:7; Ps. 127). Thus their offspring would be one (made like them), an offspring from both their makeups (Gen. 1:27–31; Ps. 127:3–5).

The Fall in the Garden

The essence of the fall of Adam and Eve in the Garden of Eden was not about good food to eat or even becoming wiser to know about good and evil. If you have such a good thing going already, why would you want to know about evil? The temptation, as the Devil had previously pursued (Isa. 14:13, 14; Mic. 6:8; Phil. 2:5, 6), was the prideful attempt to "be like God" (Gen. 3:5), which is the root of so many sins, when one thinks about it. Thus, he said, "You surely won't die" (not only going against what God said but this is a statement that only God could make; Gen. 3:4). The Devil wouldn't die physically (not being human), but he died spiritually. (By lying and usurping God's command given to Adam and Eve, he was *still* trying to "be like God.") However, both physical and spiritual deaths would occur to Adam and Eve (eventually physical death as God had said). Also worth stating, how could one become like God when one goes against His command? The result was becoming more like the schemer who deceived them.

Eve was not born yet when the command not to eat from the Tree of Knowledge of Good and Evil was given to Adam (Gen. 2:16, 17). Things to possibly better oneself both physically and mentally (not spiritually) became the focus of the temptation. The root of it, though, was rebellion toward God (usurping His authority by another) and disobeying His single prohibitive command. The result was being removed from the Garden of Eden and God's presence, which they had previously with Him (Gen. 3:24). With God's mercy, the punishments were given out to each involved (Gen. 3:14–19), and the Devil received his ultimate pronouncement (Gen. 3:15; Isa. 14:15; Matt. 25:41). But man had the hope of God's deliverance and redemption (Gen. 3:15), coming with God's seed to crush the Devil and ultimately destroy his work and bring salvation to humankind from his sins (Gal. 3).

The sin in the garden did not destroy the family but greatly disrupted it. Not only did death set in (Gen. 2:17; 3:19), but Adam and Eve were also put out of the Garden of Eden and away from God's presence (Gen. 3:8, 22–24). The first killing occurred when Cain rose up against Abel (Gen. 4:8) over a jealous response to his brother's better offerings (sacrifices) to God (Gen. 4:3–7; Heb.11:4). Abel brought to God the firstborns from his flock (Ex. 13:2; 22:29, 30; 34:19, 22, 26; Lev. 27:26). Abel also offered the fat portions of his sacrifices to the Lord, which were also required by the Lord for Israel, solely dedicating this to the Lord (Lev. 3:16, 17; 1 Sam. 2:12–17, 34, 35; 4:12–18). One wonders if God used the offerings of Abel as a model for Israel to follow (see again Heb. 11:4). Cain offered *an* offering to the Lord from the fruit of the ground (Gen. 4:3 NASB). God did not require Cain's death for the murder of his brother. Later in Noah's time God would declare this as a just judicial procedure (Gen. 9:5–7). However, Cain's punishment was still great and difficult to bear (Gen. 4:13). There was a curse upon him, yielding weak harvests after hard work in cultivating the ground. He was a vagrant and wonderer on the earth (Gen. 4:9–14). Cain also felt that he would reap what he sowed and that someone would do the same to him someday (Gen. 4:14). But God in His mercy and purpose to be fruitful and multiply on the earth (Gen. 1:28) put a mark on Cain so that this would not happen (Gen. 4:15).

And so with a beautiful beginning and a terrible disruption in the garden and following, man began to grow and populate on the earth (Gen. 4:16–26; 9:1, 7). Then, with Adam's grandson Enosh, men began to call on the name of the Lord, that is, living by His name (Gen. 4:25, 26; 5:24; 6:9).

The Family of God (Design, Model, and Applications)

God's Expansion of His Family and Desires for Them

God's has desired to expand His family by creating humankind in His image. When man enters the door that God has provided through His Son Jesus (John 10:1–11) and is born again (John 3:3–17), he becomes a child of God and enters His family (John 1:12, 13). In the complete working of harmony and compatibility of the Trinity, God works within His children to help bring about this same working in their lives with the goal of conforming to His image (nature) and maturity (Matt. 5:48; Rom. 8:28–30; 2 Cor. 3:17, 18; Eph. 4:1–13; 1 Peter 1:13–16; 2 Peter 1:2–8).

Design for the Father

As the example of our heavenly Father, God's design for the husband is to be the spiritual leader and the material provider for his family (Gen. 2:16, 17; 18:19; Deut. 4:9, 10; 6:4–9; Prov. 22:6; Eph. 5:25–33; 6:1–4). He leads and guides his wife and children (even grandchildren) to learn and live by God's Word in the Bible (Deut. 4:9; Matt. 12:46–50; Mark 10:13–16; Rom. 15:4). He leads by his caring example in nourishing and cherishing them with tender love (see 1 Thess. 2:7) as Christ does the church (Eph. 5:28, 29; Col. 3:19–21; 1 Peter 3:7).

As our Father in heaven trains His children in His ways (Deut. 4:40; 30:14–20; Ps. 32:8; Isa. 40:10, 13; 48:17; Jer. 9:23, 24; 29:11; John 14:6; 15:1, 2; 16:13; Gal. 5:22–25), fathers also have the responsibility to train their children in the ways of the Lord (Ps. 1; Prov. 1; 4; 22:6; Eccl. 12:13, 14; Eph. 6:4; Col. 3:21). Father and mother are models for their children to follow so that the proverbs become true for their children throughout their lives and their children's children who also will follow their good example (Prov. 14:26; 17:6; 20:7; 22:6; 31:10–12, 26–29; Eph. 2:10).

Discipline (for Parents and Children)

Part of training is discipline (instruction, training that corrects, molds, or perfects the mental or moral character; orderly or conduct or pattern of behavior; self-control-Merriam-Webster's Collegiate Dictionary, 11th edition, 2013). Discipline is an expression of the love of our heavenly Father for His children. Parents must help them find and stay on the narrow path of life (Matt. 7:13, 14; John 3:3–17; 10:7–10; Deut. 8:1–6; Prov. 3:5, 6, 11, 12; 2 Tim. 3:14–17; Heb. 12:4–11).

Discipline helps us to become mature (Rom. 8:12–25; Eph. 4:12–19; 5:1, 2; Heb. 12:11; 1 Peter 1:13–16; 4:12–19) and also become demonstrators of the nature of God within us (Luke 12:11, 12; John 15:1, 2, 16; Rom. 8:28–30; 12:1, 2; 1 Cor. 12:4–11; Gal. 5:16–26; Eph. 5:1, 2, 8; 1 Peter 1:14–16; 2:21–23; 2 Peter 1:2–11). It also helps do good works (John 15:12–17; Cor. 15:58–16:3; Gal. 6:7–10; Eph. 2:8–10; 4:11–13; Phil. 2:12, 13; 2 Thess. 2:16, 17; 3:13; Titus 3:8, 14; 1 Peter 2:13-21; 3:6–13, 17).

Parental Instructors

Parents likewise are to be good instructors of God's ways and moral living to their children (Deut. 4:40; 6:4–9; Ps. 78:5–7; Prov. 1:1–19;

2:1–22; 3:1–12; 4:1–27; 5:1, 2; 6:1–5, 16-26; 7:1–4, 24–27; 8:32–36; 9:6–12; 10:1; 13:1–3; 23:22–26; 31:1–31; Mark 10:13–16; Rom. 15:4–6; Eph. 6:1–4; Col. 3:18–21; 2 Tim. 3:14–17).

Sometimes the discipline is hard to carry out (Prov. 13:18–24; 15:5, 10, 12, 31–33; 19:18, 20, 25–27; 22:15, 17–21; 23:12–35; 29:3, 17). However, those trained by it will reap its benefits.

They will find the peaceful fruit (product) of righteousness (Deut. 4:35–40; 8:1–10; Job 5:17–27; Ps. 94:8–17; Prov. 6:20–23; 13:22; 22:6; 2 Cor. 12:14; Heb. 12:9–11). They will grow in the wisdom and knowledge of God (Deut. 4:1–8; Job 28:28; Prov. 1:1–9; 2:1–11; 4:1–12; 9:1–12; 15:31-33; 21:30; Eccl. 5:18–20; 7:8–12; 8:1–6; 9:13–18; 12:9–14; Isa. 11:2; Matt. 11:25–30; 25:1–13; John 16:13–15; Acts 6:1–7, 10; Rom. 16:19; 1 Cor. 1:18–2:16; James 3:13–18; compare this passage to the Beatitudes in Matthew 5:1–16.)

And as God's children loved by Him…looking forward to the blessed hope of Jesus' appearing (Titus 2:11–14) and the day when we will be with and see Him (and the Father and Holy Spirit) just as they are (1 John 3:1–3; Rev. 4; Rev. 5; Rev. 22:3–5).

Other Models of God for His Children

In the harmonious working of the Trinity and Their model for fathers and mothers raising their children here on earth, consider the following examples that the triune God lives out for His children.

God Is the One Who Guides Us into All Truth

Ex. 34:6, 7; Deut. 32:4; Ps. 25:4-10; 31:1–5; Isa. 65:16; John 1:14–18; 8:31, 32; 14:6, 16, 17, 26; 15:26; 16:13–15.

He Desires Fellowship with Us Now and Forever

Gen. 1:25–31; 3:8; Deut. 4:1-7; Ps. 16:11; 22:25–31; 23:1–6; 65:4; 100:1–5; 145:1–21; Isa. 43:1–7; 65:17–19; Jer. 9:23, 24; 31:31–33; Ezek. 37:24–28; Dan. 7:13, 14; Mark 10:13–16; John 3:14–17; 14:16, 17, 23; 17:3, 24; 2 Cor. 13:14; Heb. 12:22–24; 1 John 1:1–3; 3:1, 2; Rev. 21:1–7.

He Is Our Protector from Evil and Circumstances

Gen. 4:9–15 (Cain)
Gen. 6:13–22; 7:23; 8:20–9:7 (Noah)
Ex. 14:26–15:7 (Parting of the Red Sea)
Deut. 33:12 (Promise to Benjamin)
Josh. 6:12–21 (Capture of Jericho)
Judg. 7:19–22 (Gideon defeats Midian)

1 Sam. 1:9–11; 7:5–11 (Samuel subdues the Philistines)

1 Sam. 18:10–12; 19:8–10; 23:14 (David protected from Saul)

2 Sam. 8:1–18 (God protected and helped David in his battles for the Lord)

2 Kings 6:8–23 (Elisha and the Chariots of Fire)

2 Chron. 18:30–32; 20:1–30 (God protects Jehoshaphat and Israel)

Esther 7:1–10 (Mordecai, Esther, and the Jews are saved from death)

Jer. 26:1–24; 38:1–13 (Jeremiah protected and rescued from danger)

Isa. 37:33–38 (Israel delivered from Assyrian army threats)

Isa. 41:10–13; 43:1, 2, 8–13 (God's help and protection)

Dan. 6 (Daniel in the lion's den)

Jonah 2:1–10 (Jonah's prayer and God's protection in the belly of the fish)

Zech. 14:12–15 (God's protection of Jerusalem against those who attack it in the last days)

The Psalms

Ps. 3:3–6

Ps. 4:6–8

Ps. 10:16–18

Ps. 18:1–3

Ps. 23:4

Ps. 32:6, 7

Ps. 33:18–22

Ps. 34:1–7

Ps. 37:7–15, 39, 40

Ps. 44:4–8

Ps. 57:4–6

Ps. 61:1–4

Ps. 68:19, 20

Ps. 72:12–15

Ps. 91:1–16

Ps. 107:1–43
Ps. 118:5–9
Ps. 121:1–8
Ps. 124:1–8
Ps. 141:8–10 (a prayer)

New Testament

Matt. 6:13
Matt. 26:53
Luke 4:1–14
Luke 8:22–25
Luke 10:17–20
Luke 22:31, 32, 39–46
John 17:13–16
Acts 27:9–44
Rom. 8:26–30
1 Cor. 10:13
2 Thess. 3:3
2 Tim. 3:8–12
2 Tim. 4:16–18
Heb. 13:5, 6
1 Peter 1: 3–5
1 John 5:18–20

He Is Our Great Provider from the Beginning and Forever

Old Testament

Gen. 1:26–31
Gen. 2:18–24
Gen. 9:3
Gen. 22:1–18

Ex. 16:13–21
Num. 20:1–11
Deut. 2:7
Deut. 8:1–10
2 Sam. 23:13–17
1 Kings 5:5–10
1 Kings 17:8–24
2 Kings 7:1–20
1 Chron. 17:1–14
Neh. 2:1–8
Job.42:10–17
Ps. 23
Ps. 34:8–10
Ps. 65:9-13
Ps. 103:1–5
Ps. 107
Ps. 127 NASB
Ps. 145:8–16
Prov. 3:3–8
Eccl. 5:18–20
Isa. 12
Isa. 65:17–19
Jer. 31:31–34
Ezek. 36:26–28
Jonah 4:5, 6

New Testament

Matt. 4:24, 25
Matt. 11:28–30
Mark 6:30–44
Mark 13:9–11
Luke 7:11–16

Luke 11:1–13
Luke 12:22–34
John 1:12, 13
John 3:14–17
John 14:1–3
John 14:13–18, 23
Acts 2:43–47
1 Cor. 10:13
2 Cor. 9:6–15
Phil. 4:6–20
1 Tim. 5:17, 18
Heb. 11:13–16
Rev. 21:2–5.

He Is the Giver of Good Gifts

Gen. 1:26–28; 2:8, 9; 12:3
Deut. 4:40
Num. 11:24–30
Ex. 28:3; 39:3, 8
1 Chron. 15:22
2 Chron. 26:15; 34:8–12
1 Sam. 1:11, 20
Ruth 4:13–17
1 Kings 17:1–7, 17–24
2 Kings 6:1–7
Ps. 16:11
Ps. 23
Ps. 65:4
Ps. 84:11, 12
Ps. 103:1–5
Ps. 104

Ps. 127 NASB
Isa. 7:14; 9:6, 7
Matt. 5:43–48
Luke 11:13
John 3:16, 17
John 14:1–3
Acts 2:38, 39
Rom. 6:23
Rom. 12:3–8
1 Cor. 12:4–14; 16:1–3
2 Cor. 9:8
Eph. 4:7–13
1 Tim. 3:16
Rom. 3:21–24
2 Cor. 5:21
Phil. 3:9
1 Tim. 5:17, 18
2 Tim. 3:16, 17
Heb. 2:1–4
James 1:17, 18
1 Peter 4:10, 11
1 John 5:13–15, 18–20

God Is Our Guide and Wonderful Counselor throughout Life

Old Testament

Gen. 1:27; 2:16, 17
Deut. 30:14–20; 5:6–21
Gen. 12:1–3
Ex. 40:34–38
Num. 13:1, 2, 3, 30

Deut. 4:39, 40
Deut. 6:4–7
Deut. 29:29; 30:1–4
Josh. 1:5–9
Judg. 6:11–24
Judg. 13:1–23
1 Sam. 23:1–5
1 Kings 19:1–21
Neh. 2:1–8, 15–18
1 Chron. 17:1–15
Ps. 1
Ps. 2
Ps. 15
Ps. 16:11
Ps. 19:7–11
Ps. 23
Ps. 25:8–10
Ps. 32:8–11
Ps. 33:6–12, 18–22
Ps. 48:9–14
Ps. 67
Ps. 47:8, 9
Ps. 73:23–26
Ps. 78:5–7
Ps. 119:9–16, 105, 130
Ps. 121
Ps. 139:7–16, 23, 24
Prov. 1:1–7; 3:3–8; 4:20–27; 6:20–23; 16:3, 9; 21:30
Eccl. 8:5, 6; 20:22
Isa. 9:6, 7
Isa. 28:23–29; 40:9–14, 26, 28–31

Isa. 46:8–11

Isa. 55:6–13

Isa. 58:10, 11

Jer. 29:11

Jer. 32:17–19

Ezek. 37:24–28

Dan. 2:20, 21; 12:3, 10

Hos. 2:18–23

Amos 3:7

Ezek. 3:16, 17

Mic. 2:3–5; 6:8

Zech. 4:6–9.

New Testament

Matt. 5:1–16

Matt. 6:9–15

Matt. 7:24–29

Matt. 11:25–30

Matt. 18:1–6, 10

Luke 1:26–38, 67–79; 21:34–36

John 1:14–18

John 3:14–17, 35

John 7:37-39

John 10:1–11

John 14:6, 14–18, 26

John 16:7–15

John 17:17–21, 25

Acts 2:37-39

Acts 6:1–10

Acts 16:6–10

Rom. 8:12–17, 26–39

1 Cor. 2:1–16
1 Cor. 12:1–13
Rom. 12:3–8
Gal. 5:22–26
Phil. 2:5–16
1 Thess. 5:16–22
2 Tim. 3:16, 17
Heb. 13:7, 8
1 John 2:1, 2
Rev. 22:16, 17

While God is the God of justice, He also is the God of all comfort, compassion, mercy, and love. As one studies these characteristics, the heart of God and His love and kindness to humankind over the whole course of time to the new heaven and new earth is revealed to us. God will carry out His judgments over evil (the Book of Revelation). Since God gave of His Son, Jesus Christ, to die for the sins of humankind and offers humankind His free gift of eternal life, we truly see that God's love and mercy triumphs over judgment (Ex. 34:6, 7; 1 Kings 10:9; Jer. 31:1–3, 31–34; Mic. 7:18–20; John 3:14–17; Rom. 11:30–32; 1 Cor. 13:13; Eph. 2:11–22; James 2:12, 13; 2 Peter 3:9; Rev. 21:1–5).

The God of Justice

Old Testament

Gen. 2:16, 17; 3:17–19
Gen. 6:5–8, 13, 14
Gen. 9:5–7; 18:25
Gen. 19:15–17, 24–26
Ex. 12:12
Deut. 4:39
Ex. 14:10–31

Num. 16:1–35 (Korah's rebellion)

Deut. 1:16, 17; 4:5–8

Deut. 32:3, 4

1 Kings 3:16–28

2 Chron. 19:4–7

Ps. 9:4, 7–16

Ps. 19:9

Ps. 33:4, 5

Ps. 50:1–6, 10–12

Ps. 75; 89:14–16; 96:1–13; 99:1–9; 103:6

Ps. 111:7, 8

Ps. 140:12, 13

Ps. 146:6–10

Eccl. 12:13, 14

Isa. 2:12–22; 5:16, 17; 33:22

Isa. 9:1–7

Isa. 30:18; 42:1–4; 61:8

Isa. 45:20–25; 53:10–12

Isa. 61:4–9

Jer. 9:23, 24

Jer. 22:1–5

Jer. 32:17–20

Jer. 51:11, 24–26

Isa. 21:1–10

Hab. 1:15–2:20

Dan. 5: 24–31

Rev. 18

New Testament

Matt. 3:7–12

John 3:14–21

John 5:21–30

John 16:7–11

Rom. 1:18–20

Rom. 3:21–26

Rom. 5:18

Heb. 10:10–12

Eph. 2:4–10

Heb. 12:22–26

James 5:8, 9

1 Peter 1:14–19

1 John 2:1, 2

Rev. 6:12–17

Rev. 11:15–18

Rev. 16:4–7

Rev. 19:1–3, 11–21

Rev. 20:10–15

Rev. 21:1–7

Rev. 22:3–5

The God of All Comfort, Compassion, Mercy, and Love

Mercy—Disposition of love, respecting those in need (like compassion) and the kindly ministry of love for their relief (Unger).

Compassion—A feeling of distress through the ills of others (Vines; Neh. 9:16, 17; Jer. 31:31–34; Luke 23:33, 34; 1 John 2:1, 2).

Comfort—A calling to one's side with the capability or adaptability for giving aid (Vines); the same word for the Holy Spirit (John14:16, 26; 15:26).

Love—See previous section about the characteristics of the Trinity on God's love.

Old Testament

Gen. 1:26–31; 3:7, 21 (Adam and Eve)

Gen. 4:13–15 (Cain)

Gen. 6:7–9 (Noah)

Gen. 9:8–17 (the Rainbow)

Gen. 12:1–3; 22:18; 28:14

Acts 3:25 (Promise to Abraham, nations and families of the earth)

Gen. 14:13–16 (Abraham's victory and rescue of Lot)

Gen. 19:15–29 (Lot spared from Sodom and Gomorrah)

Gen. 24 (wife for Isaac)

Gen. 28:10–17; 32:1–32; 33:1–20 (God's mercy and blessing to Jacob)

Gen. 37:18–28; 39:19–23; 49:22–26; 50:20, 21 (God's blessings upon Joseph)

Ex. 2:1–15; 4:18–26 (Moses)

Ex. 12:21–36 (the Passover)

Ex. 14:1–15:4 (the Red Sea—Israel's deliverance from the Egyptians)

Ex. 33:17–34:8 (God's glory and declaration made known to Moses)

Deut. 6:1–9

Mark 12:28–31 (The greatest commandment)

Deut. 30:1–6 (Israel's restoration to their land)

Ruth 4:9–17 (Ruth and Naomi)

1 Sam. 18:10–12; 19:10; 23:14 (David protected from Saul)

2 Kings 6:8–23 (Chariots of fire and God's mercy on Israel and the attacking Assyrians)

2 Chron. 33:1–17 (Manasseh's repentance and God's mercy upon him)

Neh. 9:16–25, 30, 31 (God's goodness to Israel in their journey and entering the Promised Land)

1 Kings 10:9

Job 42:1–17 (Job's repentance, restoration, and blessing by God)

Isa. 37:14–38 (God's deliverance of Israel from the Assyrian king and army)

The Psalms

Ps. 6:8–10
Ps. 13:5, 6
Ps. 23
Ps. 30:10–12
Ps. 33:18–22
Ps. 36:5–9
Ps. 42:8 (prayer)
Ps. 51:16, 17
Ps. 68:5, 6
Ps. 86:5, 11–17
Ps. 100
Ps. 103
Ps. 107
Ps. 113
Ps. 118
Ps. 119:76, 77 (prayer)
Ps. 121
Ps. 127 NASB
Ps. 130:5–8
Ps. 136
Ps. 146.

Remaining Old Testament

Prov. 3:11, 12
Eccl. 5:18–20
Song of Songs 8:6, 7
Isa. 30:18
Isa. 41:10, 13
Isa. 43:1–7
Isa. 49:8-13

Isa. 54:4–10
Isa. 55:1–13
Isa. 61:1–3
Isa. 65:16–19
Jer. 31:31–34
Lam. 3:21–25
Ezek. 36:26–28
Ezek. 37:24–28
Hos. 2:18–23
Mic. 7:18–20
Zeph. 3:14–17

New Testament

Matt. 5:1–16; 9:35–37
Matt. 11:25–30
Matt. 12:7
Matt. 14:13–21
Matt. 20:29–34
Luke 7:11–17
Luke 15:11–24
Luke 22:39–46
Matt. 6:10
Luke 23:33, 34
John 3:14–17, 35
John 8:28, 29
John 11:30–45
John 14:1–3, 16–18, 23
John 15:9, 10
John 17:23, 24
Rom. 8:35–39; 9:14–26
Rom. 11:30–32
1 Cor. 13

2 Cor. 1:3–7

Gal. 5:22–25

Eph. 4:32–5:1, 2

Phil. 2:1, 2

1 Thess. 2:7, 8

1 Tim. 1:12–16

Heb. 4:14–16

James 2:12, 13; 5:10, 11

1 Peter 2:9, 10

1 John 4:7–21

Jude 20–23

Rev. 3:19–22

Rev. 21:1–7

Conclusion

As created beings by God that need to be redeemed back to God after the fall of man in the Garden of Eden, man can now come into the family of God by the born-again experience because of the death and resurrection of Jesus Christ (John 1:12, 13; 3:3–8). This is the spiritual birth brought about by God when one turns from his sins and receives the Savior, Jesus, into their life. God then gives the promised gift of the Holy Spirit as one becomes a child of God, born spiritually into His family. Through this transforming experience of going from death to life (John 5:24), we can see the remarkable things God gives us.

He gives us His life—that is, life as He has, eternal life (John 3:16; 17:3; 1 John 5:13, 20). He gives us the ability to share in His nature (2 Peter 1:2–4; Rom. 1:20). He gives and develops us so that we grow in His own character (1 Cor. 12:4–7; 2 Cor. 3:17, 18; Gal. 5:22–25; 1 John 3:1, 2). And it is God's delight to gladly give us His Kingdom (Luke 12:31, 32). The word *gladly* is the same word the angels used in proclaiming the Savior's coming to earth in Luke 2:14 (KJV).

With God giving so much of Himself and what He creates for us, how can we not be thankful to Him and not want to grow more and more in His likeness? (Isa. 65:17–19; 2 Cor. 3:17, 18; Eph. 4:11–16; 5:1, 2). Remember the temptation in the Garden of Eden. The new birth through our growth and into completion in heaven is the work of God, that comes to us by grace (His gift to us) through our faith in Him

(John 1:12, 13; 1 Cor. 12:6; Eph. 2:8, 9; Phil. 2:5–13; 1 John 3:2). Now as His redeemed children, how can we not want to serve Him as His faithful priests that He has made us to be? (Dan. 7:13, 14; Rom. 12:1, 2; 1 Peter 2:9, 10; Rev. 1:4–6; 5:9, 10; 20:6). Such is and will be our role in the privilege of ever-serving almighty God in His everlasting kingdom. He has given us His life and so much of Himself, and what He has made for us to enjoy with Him (Isa. 65:17–19; Rev. 7:15–17; 21:1–3; 22:1–5).

Then will the greatest commandment be fulfilled (and forever enjoyed) (Deut. 6:4, 5; 10:12–14; Lev. 19:18; Mark 12:28–31), through the great work of the Trinity (Eph. 3:14–19), as we come to know and grow and experience how much God truly love us (1 Kings 10:9; Isa. 43:1–7; Isa. 65:17–19; Jer. 31:1–3, 31–34; Ezek. 37:24–28; Hos. 2:17–23; 11:1–4; John 3:15–17; 13:1; 14:15–18, 23; 15:9, 13–15; 17:24–26; Eph. 1:3–6; 3:17–19; 1 John 3:1, 2; 4:7–21; Rev. 21:1–7).

All this, from the very beginning into all eternity, coming from the heart of God for us (Gen. 1:26–31; 3:15; 12:1–3; 22:14–18; 28:12–15; 1 Chron.17:9–14; Neh.9:9–31; Ps. 2; Isa.25:1; Jer. 9:23, 24; 31:13–34; 32:38–41; Hos. 2:18–23; John 1:1, 2, 16–18; 3:16, 17; 16:33; 17:24; 1 Cor. 13:12, 13; 15:47–53; Eph. 5:1, 2; 2 Peter 3:8–13; Rev. 21:1–3).

It is done fully to God's great delight (Isa. 65:17–19; Jer. 32:38–41; Ezek. 34:23–31; 37:24–28; Zeph. 3:14–17; Zech. 14:9; Ex. 20:1–6; Deut. 4:32–39; John 17:24–26; Rev. 21:1–3; 22:3–5);

And will be complete when the family of God will be together with the Father, the Son, and the Holy Spirit forever (Ps. 16:11; 22:27, 28; Ezek. 37:24–28; 43:7–9; Heb. 12:22–24; Rev. 4; Rev. 5; Rev. 21:3) and evermore (Ps.65:4; Rev.22:3-5; Ps.84:4).

Bibliography

Strong, James; Strong's Exhaustive Concordance of the Bible; Public Domain.

Unger, Merrill F; The New Unger's Bible Dictionary; Harrison, R.K., Edit; Vos, Howard F and Barber, Cyril J., Contrib. Edit.; Chicago; Moody Press, 1988.

Vine, W.E.; Vine's Expository Dictionary of New Testament Words; Nashville, TN; Thomas Nelson, Inc.; 1940; all rights reserved; reprinted by permission.

By permission. From Merriam-Webster's Collegiate® Dictionary, 11th Edition, ©2013 by Merriam-Webster, Inc. (www.Merriam-Webster.com).

All reprints used by permission of the publishers.